DESERT BRATS

Created by
Harry Markos & Andy Briggs

Written by
Harry Markos

Art by
Melissa Capriglione

Edited by
Ian Sharman

THE KONCEPT FACTORY

MARKOSIA

ISBN 978-1-915387-21-9

www.markosia.com

This is planet Earth one thousand years from now.

It is a sandy, barren planet with tiny pockets of water.

With almost no water there is very little life remaining.

Earth was a lush planet with much water and millions of different life forms.

Our ancestors' greed and selfish nature left it a desolate planet.

Almost everything was destroyed as a result. In time the planet became one large desert wasteland.

Fortunately there were some hardy species who were able to survive the catastrophe.

Small animals who were used to tough terrain and desert climates were able to survive.

They evolved over the centuries and now rule what is left.

Simarra is one of the last surviving towns on the planet.

High protective walls were built to protect the town from bandits.

Over time the desert sand has piled up high against the walls.

The walls were built to protect the rare lake as well as the inhabitants.

Water is precious and there is so little left that it is a priceless treasure.

The town formed the Desert Rats to protect them, which they have done so for many generations.

They patrol the town and the surrounding desert for signs of bandits.

Without the Desert Rats the bandits would have taken over decades ago.

Every citizen has to serve some time in the Desert Rats, it is their civic duty to do so.

This is Merv, our... *hero*.

Merv usually looks like this, upset about something or other.

Today he is somewhat sad because he has toothache... and a stomach ache... and possibly an infection... of something or other.

Merv is like this all the time - he always seems to think there is something wrong with him.

Almost all of the time there isn't anything wrong with him at all.

Karlo is one of Merv's best friends. He doesn't have many!

"Hey Merv, whatcha doing today?" he asks.

"Hi Karlo. I'm off on patrol again in a few minutes. We're going out a long way today."

"Sounds like fun, make sure you look out for some human stuff for me!"

"I will do," replies Merv, sniffling from his mysterious 'infection'. "If I can last the pace."

Karlo knows better than to say anything about his friend's phantom illnesses, and waves goodbye.

The Desert Rats have been patrolling for many hours.

They are in an area that hasn't been visited for many years, because of rumours that bandits are in the region.

The bandits have been causing many problems of late and the townsfolk are worried, which is why there are now extra patrols.

They need to drive the bandits away from Simarra.

Merv spots a bandit spying on them!

"It's a bandit! It's a bandit!" he cries out.

Merv chases Streak, the slippery bandit, but doesn't look where he is going.

He runs over some rotten wood which has been placed to hide the bandits' precious secret water supply.

The bandit slithers away as Merv's friend stumbles into the well!

He manages to grab on to something to stop falling in.

"Hold on!" says Merv as he tries to pull him to safety.

The rest of the troop rush in to help.

Many of them look at Merv disapprovingly, as if blaming him for the accident.

They are, of course, quite right to do so!

But Merv is clumsy, and as he pulls the legionnaire to safety he kicks over part of the wall.

The wall collapses towards the troop and into the well. Everyone scatters out of the way.

Merv bumps his head upon falling.

Merv looks up, his head spinning from the fall.

He sees what looks like a spectacular city of twinkling turrets floating in the sky.

The image is hazy and looks unreal and Merv thinks he is imagining it.

"Strange," he says out loud, "that looks like the city on the Elder's medallion."

The other troopers cannot see anything as the mirage suddenly vanishes, and nobody believes him.

Streak explains to the dreaded Eli Baba, leader of the desert bandits, that the Desert Rats have discovered their secret well, one of their few precious sources of water.

"That's all we need," he shouts, "now we have to look for a new well!"

In an attempt to sooth his anger, Streak tells Eli about Merv's vision, which he had seen.

Eli's expression changes from one of anger to one of interest.

"The legends say that the lost treasure of Ali Baba is hidden in the sacred City," he says.

"You must go back and find out where it is!" he demands of Streak.

Merv meets with his friends Virgil, Karlo and Jamila, who he has a soft spot for.

He explains to them what he had seen earlier in the day.

"It was there, I tell you! A city in the sky with turrets and everything!"

Virgil says, "Weird, that sounds like the same city that is pictured on the Elder's medallion."

Virgil then tells the friends the legend of Ali Baba and his famous treasure that was hidden in the sparkling city in the sky.

"I read about it in a book," he adds. "There was a carving on one of the pages that is identical to the medallion."

Suddenly a loud burst of noise interrupts the gathering as two Desert Rats walk briskly nearby, blowing the call to arms, a call for citizens that an important announcement is about to be made.

Karlo is the first to speak, intrigued by the fuss.

"I wonder what that's all about," he says to the others.

"There hasn't been a call to arms for years," adds Jamila, concerned that something like this is only likely to be bad news.

"I'm sure it's not as serious as you think," adds Virgil, despite the fact that he is suddenly as nervous as the others.

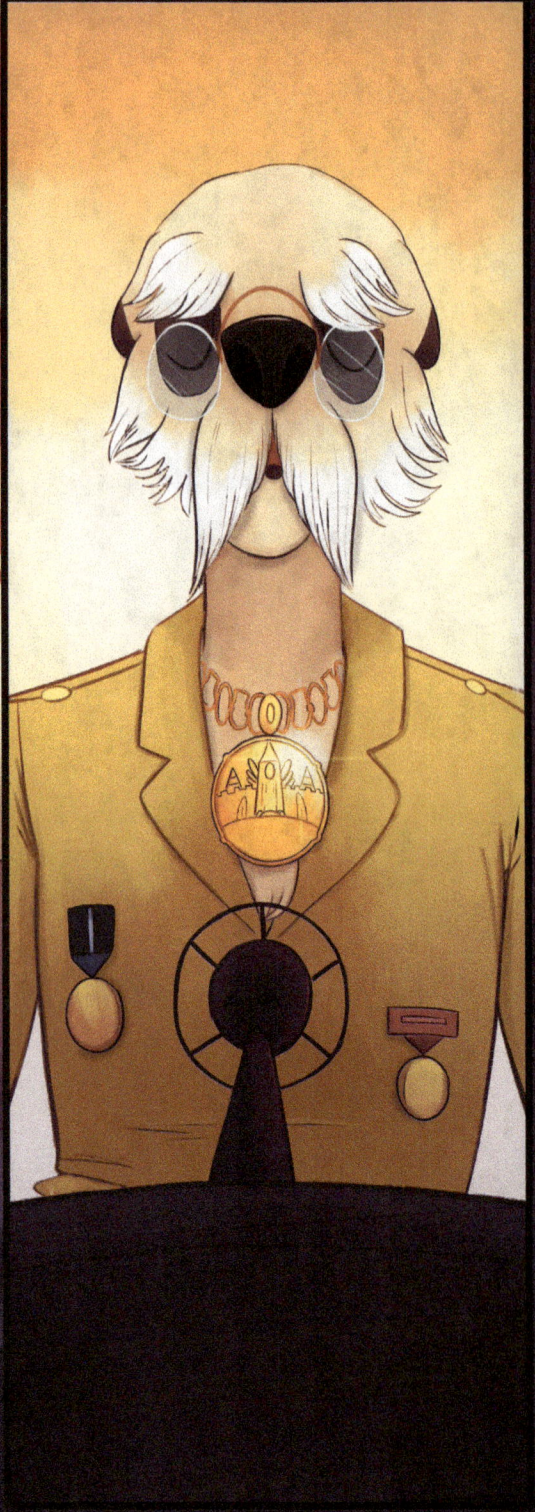

The people are quiet as the Elder speaks, a respectful hush falls for their leader.

"The bandit raids are becoming more frequent," he calls out. "We are managing to hold them back, thanks to the courage of the Desert Rats, but our time here grows short."

The people are stunned at these words and await an explanation.

"The sands of the desert have almost breached the walls, and our water levels are running low. We must take flight soon and seek another place to live. We must abandon the city or we will perish!"

Merv, stunned by the announcement, suddenly notices the medallion around Elbert's neck.

"Look," he shouts, pointing towards the podium, "that's exactly what I saw in the sky earlier!"

Karlo, a deep thinker at the best of times, doesn't believe that this is a coincidence and asks Merv some questions, probing for answers.

Karlo says to Merv, "If you are right about the city then it could be the place that we need to go to save Simarra! What else can you remember?"

Merv thinks hard about his vision, hoping to remember more.

"I can't think of anything right now, Karlo. Maybe once I sleep on it something will come back."

The sly bandit Streak listens to every word as he spies from behind a market stall.

Streak uses his cunning to move around the town unseen as he hatches a plan to get more information.

He waits for his contact in the town to signal so that he can get into the compound where he plans to steal the medallion!

"That medallion is the key to the treasure," he thinks to himself, "and Eli will reward me handsomely if I can get it for him."

He sees the signal that he has been waiting for, coming from a darkened window where there are no guards patrolling.

"Here we go," he says as he slithers towards the traitor's signal.

Streak slithers into the room to see his contact, the traitor Ramone!

The trusted adviser to the Elder harbours ambitions to rule the town, and he needs the help of Eli Baba and his murderous bandits.

He tells Streak where to go to steal the medallion.

"And remember," Ramone adds, "once you have the medallion you must leave via the North gate. And tell Eli Baba that I will be in touch soon."

"That is the elder's room where you will find the medallion" says Ramone to Streak, "remember that once you have stolen it you must leave immediately, otherwise our plan of blaming this on a Desert Rat will be jeopardised."

Streak smirks as he slides towards the bedroom. Within seconds he has stolen the priceless medallion and within minutes he has slithered from the town and into the darkness.

"Somebody help! Come quickly! We are all doomed!" shouts the distressed Elder, Elbert, who has discovered that the precious medallion has been stolen.

The medallion has been in the charge of the Elders for many generations and is said to be the key to the safety of Simarra.

Elbert is dreading what may now happen.

Ramone and Captain Cray report to the elder that Merv had been heard speaking about the medallion the previous day. Ramone, seeking the opportunity to blame someone for the theft, angrily orders Captain Cray to arrest Merv immediately.

Merv is dragged in front of the elders and his superiors and challenged about the theft of the medallion.

He tries to explain about the mirage that he had seen but nobody will believe him.

Ramone, knowing full well that Merv is innocent, points towards the jail.

He says, "You are a liar and a thief and you have endangered our town. Take him away!"

Within minutes poor innocent Merv is locked behind bars!

Merv knows that nobody will believe him and decides to break out of jail.

"I have to prove my innocence, and the only way to do that is to find the medallion and bring it back."

He looks around and decides to head back to the old well where he first saw the mirage.

Jamila is on duty and sees Merv trying to escape. She confronts him and calls for Karlo and Virgil who are hiding around the corner.

"I'm innocent!" says Merv. "Someone has set me up, it wasn't me!"

Jamila begins to believe Merv when Karlo and Virgil remember having seen a snake-like shadow leaving the town, towards the bandits' hideout.

"Okay, let's go and get it back then!" says Jamila to the delight of them all.

The friends start walking towards bandit territory, hoping to encounter the dreaded bandits and steal back the medallion. Their journey is slow though, but luckily they come across some traders camped in the desert, next to a shiny sleek sand yacht!

"If we could somehow 'borrow' that sand yacht we could get the medallion back so much quicker!" says the devious Karlo.

"Woo hoo!" they all shout as the sand yacht almost flies along the desert floor, taking the friends far from the traders and closer to the bandits.

Unfortunately for the friends the bandits can see them coming for miles.

They prepare a trap for the sand yacht and it's unsuspecting passengers in order to delay them.

The sand yacht strikes the hidden barricade and the friends are hurled out and onto the desert floor.

Without transport the friends are left stranded in the desert with nothing for miles around.

The friends start walking. After many hours they are all very tired, hungry and especially thirsty. There is nothing to see for miles around and they begin to doubt whether they will find anything. It appears that they are doomed!

Suddenly Merv hears laughter! He looks up towards the sound and sees two vultures sitting on a dead tree.

"What did you do, forget to fly?" asks one of the vultures as they both continue to laugh at the friends.

"Yeah," says the other one, "cos if you could fly you'd be able to see the ancient city, but you can't!"

The other vulture hits his friend on the back of the head.

"Idiot! Now they know about the city and we can't have any more fun!"

"Wow!" says Jamila. "This place is amazing!"

"This is the city from the mirage!" exclaims Merv, excitedly.

Virgil points down towards a distant figure running into the ruined city.

"Look!" he shouts.

"We must be getting close," says Karlo. "Let's go!"

The friends descend and enter the city, hoping for a short and successful visit.

Unfortunately for the friends they have entered the bandits' lair!

They are quickly surrounded and captured.

"Don't panic," says the brave Jamila, "we'll find a way out of this."

"We have to," replies the frightened Merv, "otherwise Simarra is doomed!"

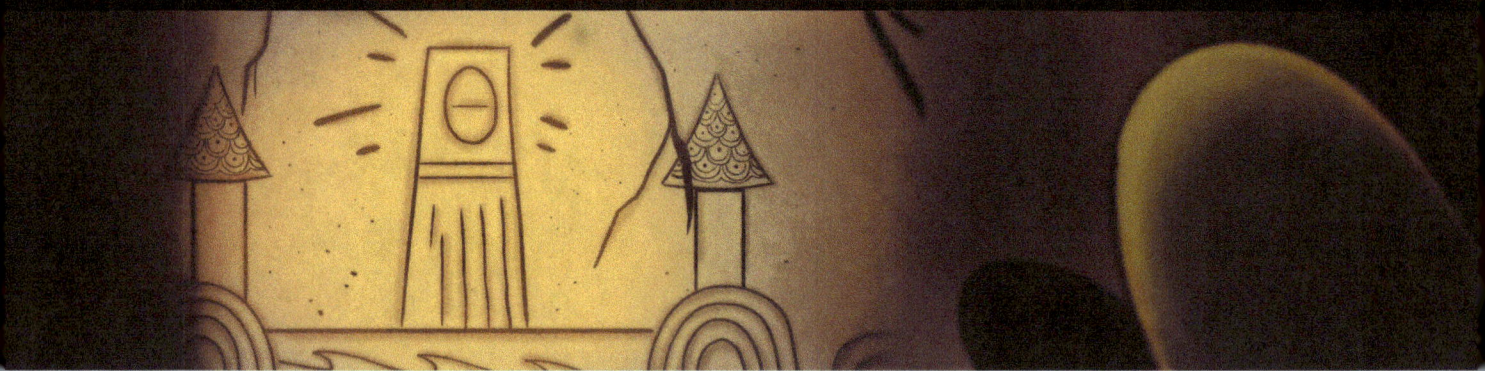

Eli Baba is angry! He holds up the precious medallion and shouts, "you know where the treasure is, and you're going to show me how to find it!"

Merv explains that they don't know exactly, which is why they're there.

He then sees the murals on the wall and after studying them shouts in triumph!

"The treasure is back in Simarra! It's always been there, right under our feet!"

Suddenly, hidden traps placed there many years ago are activated by the groups presence.

The room trembles and shakes as it starts to fall apart, threatening the safety of the group.

Eli Baba sees the threat and runs away quickly, clutching the precious medallion.

Merv sees the bandit leader running away and realizes that the safety of his people depends on him retrieving the medallion.

The city is destroyed by the ancient traps.

Merv, Karlo and Virgil are missing, presumed lost to the destruction.

Jamila is still a prisoner of Eli Baba, who will use her as a bargaining tool when he returns to Simarra to claim the fabled treasure.

Jamila is devastated that her friends are missing, especially Merv, and she fears the worst.

Our heroes are still very much alive though!

They have fallen into the ruins and are holding on to a wooden beam for their lives, trying to figure a way out of the mess.

"Try not to move," Merv says quietly, "while we think of a way out of here."

Suddenly, due to the swirling dust, Virgil sneezes loudly!

The wooden beam creaks and then finally surrenders, plummeting into the darkness below.

They land in an underground river, which takes them far underground and eventually beaches them near the exit to the cave.

Merv and Karlo look at Virgil, who is feeling guilty that his sneeze was responsible for their rapid and eventful trip underground.

"Sorry, I couldn't help it," he says meekly.

Karlo looks around and spots a light in the distance.

"Look," he says, "a way out. We need to get back to Simarra quickly, before it's too late!"

The bandits reach Simarra and hatch a plan to steal the treasure.

The traitor, Ramone, lets them in through a deserted side gate.

Fortunately, Sergeant Mallory did not trust Ramone and was keeping an eye on him. He saw the traitor let the bandits into the city.

"Just as I thought," he says, "Merv was innocent all along! I'm going to need some help here."

Out in the desert the friends are captured by Captain Cray and his men.

They are happy to have been caught because it means that they can get back to Simarra quickly. Merv explains what happened in the desert with the bandits and Jamila's capture.

Captain Cray is bemused, wondering why Merv is so happy.

"Maybe he was innocent all along?" he asks himself.

They make their way back to Simarra at double time.

Ramone leads the bandits to Elbert's house. Very quickly they overpower and capture the Elder.

Ramone dons the Elder's robe and declares himself the new elder of Simarra.

Eli Baba dangles the medallion in front of Elbert and demands the location of the treasure.

Elbert is defiant and says nothing.

Eli Baba then threatens to kill Jamila if he doesn't give them the location.

Captain Cray and his men watch in disbelief as the bandits lead Jamila and Elbert away.

"So Merv was right," he says. "Simarra is under threat and Ramone was the traitor all along!"

He calls his men over and tells them what to do.

Cray and the friends quickly over-power Ramone as he is about to settle down for his first night as the new Elder, a reign that doesn't last very long!

"Where are they taking Jamila and Elbert," Merv demands angrily.

"You are too late," Ramone replies defiantly, "they're on their way to claim the secret treasure under the island."

The bandits enter the ancient tower and head towards the treasure, excited that their quest is almost over.

Merv and his friends watch them from a distance, worried that they might be too late.

"I must save Jamila," thinks Merv, not realizing that the last few days have made him brave and fearless for the first time in his life.

The bandits finally reach their destination, the fabled treasure room!

Only there doesn't appear to be any way in! Eli Baba looks around angrily, searching for a way in so that he can claim his treasure.

Elbert knows that the only way in is to speak the ancient words in a certain way, something that he cannot do himself, as he is tone deaf!

Merv and his friends catch up with the bandits before they can enter the treasure room, and they face off angrily.

Eli Baba does the only thing he knows will make Merv back down, he threatens Jamila.

Merv reluctantly relents and agrees to help Eli Baba enter the treasure room, in exchange for the safe return of Jamila and Elbert.

He takes the medallion from Eli Baba and looks at the inscription, before singing towards the door the secret words: "Says you, says me: says open sesame."

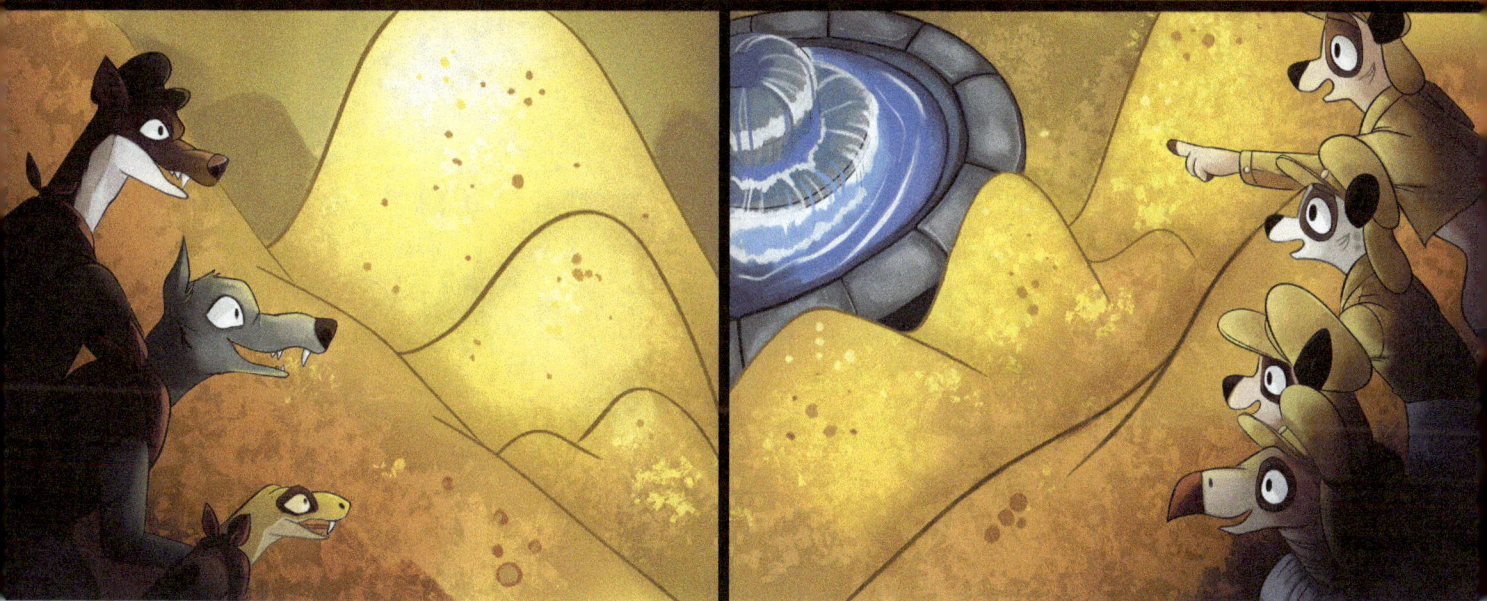

The door opens slowly, to reveal an amazing sight!

In the centre of the room is a huge fountain, flowing from the floor high up towards the ceiling. The source of all the water in the area!

Surrounding the fountain is the largest pile of treasure you could possibly imagine, gems and gold of all sizes and descriptions.

The bandits rush towards the gold and jewels – and immediately set off traps that have been hidden for centuries!

Water streams into the treasure room at a rapid rate, sweeping many of the bandits away.

The spirits that guard the treasure circle the room, making sure that everyone who has entered is chased away.

Karlo and Virgil grab Jamila and Elbert and pull them to safety as the water cascades past them.

Merv tries to join them but is grabbed by the defiant Eli Baba, who pulls him under as they 're both swept away by the water.

Eli Baba pulls Merv under the water, determined to hold on to his foe as they fight.

Suddenly, he spots a glint of treasure below and decides that treasure is more valuable than a prisoner. He lets go of Merv and swims down to claim his prize, forgetting that he can't breathe under water!

The curse has been lifted and the water that has been safely hidden for countless generations is finally released to the world!

The residents of Simarra watch in awe as the water flows out of the ancient tower.

Karlo, Virgil and Jamila are amongst the crowd, watching the spectacle before them, wondering whether they will ever see Merv again.

After what seems like an age, the friends, fearful for his safety, see Merv emerge from the lake. Wet, exhausted, but safe!

They run to their friend and hug him until their arms hurt.

It is only then that Jamila kisses Merv, the hero of Simarra!

www.ingramcontent.com/pod-product-compliance
Lightning Source LLC
LaVergne TN
LVHW081449070426
835508LV00016B/1420